the agent

for Piergiorgio Nicolazzini
who did what he said

MARTIN WAGNER is a writer and film-maker living in London. His science-fiction novel *Rachel's Machine* was published by Pinter & Martin in the UK and by Mondadori in Italy.

In 2003 he published the acclaimed *The Little Driver*, which is used in Spain to educate children about traffic issues. This was followed in 2005 by *The Little Politician*, a biting satire on contemporary British politics.

His films include the short films *Summer* and *The Subtitles,* and the documentary *Klaus Maria Brandauer: Speer in London.*

The Agent is his first play.

the agent

martin wagner

pinter & martin

PINTER & MARTIN

The Agent

First published in Great Britain by Pinter & Martin Ltd 2007

ISBN 978-1-905177-13-4

British Library Cataloguing-in-Publication Data
A catalogue record for this book is available from the British Library.

Set in Bembo

Printed in Great Britain by
TJ International Ltd, Padstow, Cornwall

Printed on chlorine-free paper. The paper used for the text of this book
is FSC certified. The Forest Stewardship Council is an international
network to promote responsible management of the world's forests.

Pinter & Martin Ltd
6 Effra Parade
London SW2 1PS

www.pinterandmartin.com

The Agent was first performed at
The Old Red Lion Theatre, London,
on March 6th 2007

ALEXANDER   Hamish Clark
STEPHEN Stephen Kennedy

Voice of CHARLIE   Lee Boardman

Director Lesley Manning
Set Designer Humphrey Jaeger
Stage Manager Peter Mazurkovic
Casting director Sarah Bird
Poster design Thorsten Knaub

Produced by Pinter & Martin Ltd

for The Old Red Lion
Artistic Director Helen Devine

Many thanks to Helen Devine and all the staff at The Old Red Lion, Guy Chapman, Will Maidwell and Jenny Eldridge at GCA, Gilly Sanguinetti, Bogus Machnik, Richard Boyd, the National Film & Television School, Christie, Bill Norris at Central Books, Candid Arts Trust, Esther Vilar, Fr Peter Andrews of St Thomas', Robbie Kelly and Janet Hadwin.

CHARACTERS

ALEXANDER
A successful agent, late 30s.

STEPHEN
An unsuccessful writer, early 40s.

TIME

Present.

LOCATION

The agent's office.

ACT I

Bright morning sunshine streams through the open venetian blinds of a tastefully decorated, modern office. The walls are lined with bookshelves, which are bursting at the seams. A single large desk stands in front of the window.

A few framed posters, advertising highbrow but popular books, line the wall wherever a gap in the bookshelves allows. From beyond the door we can hear the sound of an open-plan office – the occasional ringing of a phone, the odd subdued voice.

ALEXANDER enters the room and closes the door behind him, shutting out the noise. In his late thirties, dressed in comfortable, casual but expensive clothes, he places his briefcase next to his desk.

He sits down in his chair, presses a button on the keyboard of his computer.

Nothing happens.

He tries again, and gets increasingly frustrated when the computer doesn't start up. Finally he awkwardly gets on his knees and climbs under the desk, fiddling with the power leads for the computer, but to no avail.

When the intercom buzzes, ALEXANDER bangs his head on the desk.

ALEXANDER   Shit.
            (*The intercom buzzes again.* ALEXANDER *climbs out from underneath the desk, irritated.*

It buzzes again.)
Christ! (ALEXANDER *presses his intercom.*)
Yes.

MALE VOICE   (*on intercom*) A Stephen Parker to see you.
Says he's got an appointment.

ALEXANDER   (*to himself, obviously having forgotten*) Shit. (*he thinks, presses button, into intercom*) Where's Samantha?

MALE VOICE   (*on intercom*) Not here.

ALEXANDER   (*to himself*) I can see that. (*presses button, into intercom*) Send him in. (ALEXANDER *climbs under the desk again. After a short while there's a timid knock at the door.*) Come in. (*There's another knock at the door, this time a little louder.*) Come in!

ALEXANDER *reluctantly starts to climb out from under the desk again, when the door opens.* STEPHEN *enters. He can only be an unsuccessful writer, cheaply dressed and not at all comfortable with himself. Despite the lines of books, he looks out of place in these plush surroundings.*

ALEXANDER   Hi, Steve.

STEPHEN   Sorry I'm late.

ALEXANDER   Quite all right.

STEPHEN   I got stuck in traffic.

ALEXANDER   I spent half an hour trying to find a place to park.

STEPHEN   I came by bus.

ALEXANDER   (*ignores him*) Lost my car-park pass. It's a bloody nightmare getting another one.

ACT I

STEPHEN *looks around the room.*
ALEXANDER *moves back behind his desk.*

ALEXANDER   Just a mo. I just got in myself.

ALEXANDER *occupies himself with the computer again.*

STEPHEN *has begun to scan the bookshelves.*
ALEXANDER *has climbed under the desk
again and is fiddling with his computer;*
STEPHEN *takes a book from the shelf.*

*He opens it gently, careful not to break the
spine, and smells it.*

STEPHEN   I love the smell of new books.
(ALEXANDER *glances up at* STEPHEN *briefly,
but ignores the remark.* STEPHEN *replaces the
book on the shelf, picks another.*)
Have you read them all?
ALEXANDER   They're our authors.
STEPHEN   Just for fun?
ALEXANDER   I read first drafts, tenth drafts, outlines, syn-
opses, whatever. The finished books? (*shrugs
his shoulders*) There just isn't time.
STEPHEN   You must feel a great sense of satisfaction.
ALEXANDER   (*gets up from underneath his desk*) What?
STEPHEN   Your books. Most writers manage no more
than this much . . . (STEPHEN *indicates the
space of a foot of books with his hand, or a
dozen volumes, then points at the shelves*) You

have all these.

ALEXANDER   That's one way of looking at it. (*he tries the computer again*).

STEPHEN   I can hardly find the time these days.

ALEXANDER   (*not interested*) For what?

STEPHEN   Reading.

ALEXANDER   Oh.

STEPHEN   Ironic, isn't it?

ALEXANDER   (*absent-mindedly*) Yes.

STEPHEN   All your life you want to work with literature, and when you're finally doing it, you can hardly find the time to read.
(STEPHEN *picks up a paperback book from a row of identical ones.* ALEXANDER *notices.*)

ALEXANDER   Our bestseller, would you believe. Not my cup of tea, but who's complaining? The numbers are just unbelievable.

STEPHEN   Been meaning to get a copy. (*when there's no sign from* ALEXANDER *that he can take it,* STEPHEN *replaces the book in the shelf along with a dozen copies of the same book.*)

ALEXANDER   Just sold his new one to the States for one point five.

STEPHEN   Million?

ALEXANDER   And that's just for starters.

STEPHEN   Not bad.

ALEXANDER   Not bad for *two pages*. (STEPHEN *looks at* ALEXANDER, *perplexed*.) A two-page outline, that's all it took. It was just one of those times where everything clicked. They wanted to buy, we wanted to sell. I went in for the kill. Paperback and movie rights still to come.

STEPHEN   Seems like half the books are written to be turned into movies these days. It's hard to find a book that hasn't got any good 'scenes' in it.

ALEXANDER   Forever the purist.

STEPHEN   But imagine getting a million.

ALEXANDER   One point five.

STEPHEN   Imagine getting that kind of money as an advance. I don't know what I'd do. (*turns to* ALEXANDER) I bet he's suffering from writer's block.

ALEXANDER   He's already halfway through. E-mailed the first twelve chapters last night.

(STEPHEN *looks dejected.* ALEXANDER, *trying to make his computer work, quickly groans in frustration.*)

Do you know anything about computers?

STEPHEN   A thing or two.

ALEXANDER   I'll have to get Samantha to get someone in to fix it. (ALEXANDER *wiggles some more connections. Finally the computer makes a start-up noise.*) Ah, here we go. (ALEXANDER *presses a few keys.*) I'll just be a sec . . .

(STEPHEN *notices some books on the bottom shelf, kneels down to investigate.*)

STEPHEN   You still have copies of my book.

ALEXANDER   We do?

STEPHEN   I have only one copy left myself. Only got half a dozen to begin with.

ALEXANDER   Take them. (STEPHEN *doesn't want to understand.*) Your books. Take them. They're probably more use to you than to us.

STEPHEN   I couldn't.

ALEXANDER I don't mind. Plenty of books here. Don't have the room for them. Our clients will start to think we don't send out these things, just hoard them.
(STEPHEN *contemplates taking a copy of his book, but seems uncomfortable with the idea.*)
To be entirely frank, we're just going to throw them out.
(STEPHEN *doesn't know what to make of it. He reluctantly takes a copy, then hesitates.*)
Go on.

STEPHEN If you're sure.

ALEXANDER (*impatiently*) I'm sure.
(STEPHEN *takes his bag, and stuffs it awkwardly with several copies of his book. He leaves two copies of the book, gets up again.*)
(ALEXANDER *seems to be reading his email, while* STEPHEN *awkwardly stands there, his overfilled bag in his hand.* ALEXANDER finally notices.*)
Take a seat.
(STEPHEN *sits down, puts his bag next to his chair on the floor.*)
(ALEXANDER *scans a few messages, seems pleased for a second, but doesn't share anything with* STEPHEN. *Finally he presses a couple of keys.*)
Sorry. (*He swivels his seat towards* STEPHEN)
I'm all yours. (*shuffles through some papers*)
Sorry about cancelling last week.

STEPHEN How did it go?

ALEXANDER Fine. Jake Mac just needed some hand-holding.

STEPHEN	Jake Mackenzie?
ALEXANDER	Yes.
STEPHEN	I didn't know you represented him.
ALEXANDER	No one knows. We just took him on.
STEPHEN	Congratulations.
ALEXANDER	Stepped off the plane at 8 am. Did thirty-two interviews. Left at 8 pm.
STEPHEN	That's OK. It was my daughter's birthday anyway.
ALEXANDER	Jake and I go back years. Been after him for a while, but he's a piece of work. High maintenance, but he's worth it.
STEPHEN	I bet.
ALEXANDER	You wouldn't believe what these people are like.
STEPHEN	What people?
ALEXANDER	People who could publish their shopping lists. While the rest of us have to work for a living.
	(*There's an awkward pause. Both expect the other to speak.*)
	So, what can I do for you?
STEPHEN	(*puzzled*) You said I should come and see you. That we should have a chat.
ALEXANDER	Yes.
STEPHEN	About the book.
ALEXANDER	That's right. The book. The book. I read it again.
STEPHEN	You did?
ALEXANDER	Yes. Since the last time we spoke . . .
STEPHEN	Tuesday.
ALEXANDER	Yes, Tuesday.
STEPHEN	Today is only Thursday.

ALEXANDER   Why is it so important? Since the last time we spoke on the telephone.

STEPHEN   I'm flattered you took the time. (ALEXANDER *ignores him*) And? What do you think of it?

ALEXANDER   (*leans back, looks* STEPHEN *in the eyes.*) What do *you* think of it?

STEPHEN   Well, I don't know.

ALEXANDER   (*quick*) I don't know either.

STEPHEN   It's . . . I don't know. I'm so close to it.

ALEXANDER   Of course you are. You just finished it.

STEPHEN   Four months ago.

ALEXANDER   It's been four months already?

STEPHEN   I haven't looked at it for a while.

ALEXANDER   Read it. Sit down and read it.

STEPHEN   I don't know whether I can.

ALEXANDER   Give it a try.

STEPHEN   (*cautiously*) I'm quite happy with it. Generally.

ALEXANDER   (*disappointed*) I see.

STEPHEN   Don't you think it's . . . ?

ALEXANDER   I don't know.

STEPHEN   To be honest . . .

ALEXANDER   Yes?

STEPHEN   I really *am* quite happy with it.

ALEXANDER   I see. (*shuffles through his papers.*)

STEPHEN   It wasn't easy.

ALEXANDER   It never is.

STEPHEN   It may need revisions.

ALEXANDER   (*quick*) I agree.

STEPHEN   Here and there.

ALEXANDER   Yes. I felt that.

STEPHEN   (*sizes up* ALEXANDER *carefully.*) But I think

	it's almost there. The story, the characters...
ALEXANDER	It's certainly an improvement on the last one.
STEPHEN	I thought you liked the last one?
ALEXANDER	I did.
STEPHEN	Good reviews.
ALEXANDER	No sales.
STEPHEN	But it was published.
ALEXANDER	For no advance.
STEPHEN	A first book.
ALEXANDER	Yes.
STEPHEN	But?
ALEXANDER	But . . . it was lacking something.
STEPHEN	It was a first novel. And I don't think . . .
ALEXANDER	I like this one better.
	(ALEXANDER *looks deep in thought*.)
STEPHEN	Yes?
ALEXANDER	I just thought of something.
STEPHEN	Yes?
ALEXANDER	Sorry, it's for Jake. Just let me make a note . . . before I forget. (*he scribbles something on a notepad*) My memory's like a sieve. (*he finishes, looks up at STEPHEN again*) By the way, I made some notes. Thought you might be interested. On your typescript. I had Samantha print it out. I hope you don't mind. I have it here somewhere.
STEPHEN	Notes?
ALEXANDER	Just suggestions. Don't take them personally.
STEPHEN	But they are about *my* book?
ALEXANDER	Of course. (*searches on his desk for the typescript*.) There it is. (*retrieves something, scans*

it) Nope. (*he looks in another pile. The search is fruitless*) It is a very good read, really. Wonderful. It just has a couple of – what shall we call them? – *things* in it I'm not entirely happy with.

STEPHEN (*cautiously*) Like what?

ALEXANDER Just a few questions that remain . . . unanswered. (*looks at* STEPHEN) Who is the protagonist? What does he learn? Why does the story change focus? What *is* the story? As I said I made some notes . . . on the typescript. I hope you don't mind.

STEPHEN Not at all.

ALEXANDER After all, that's what I'm here for. To cut out the dead wood . . .

STEPHEN Dead wood?

ALEXANDER You know I like your writing. It's . . . *interesting*. There are just a few things that are too . . . *clever*. Clever is good, but you know what I mean. Just a few things. My notes should be . . .

(ALEXANDER *starts looking for the typescript again, but quickly gives up when the intercom buzzes.*)

(*presses button, into intercom*) Yes?

MALE VOICE (*on intercom*) A Malcolm Harris on line one.

ALEXANDER (*into intercom*) Thanks. (*to* STEPHEN) Now, *his* manuscript. That *does* need work. (*picks up phone*) Hi, Mal . . . Not quite through yet . . . But looking good . . . Why don't you . . . why don't you and Allie come round this weekend and we'll have a chat

about where to go with it? . . . Sounds
great . . . See you . . . Love to Allie. (*puts
the phone down, makes a quick note and turns
back to* STEPHEN.) Where were we? . . .

STEPHEN My book.

ALEXANDER Yes, your characters.

STEPHEN Yes?

ALEXANDER They're a little – now don't take offence –
a little . . .

STEPHEN Yes?

ALEXANDER How shall I put this . . . ? They are a little
. . . *unreal.*

STEPHEN Unreal?

ALEXANDER Yes.

STEPHEN They're all based on people I know.

ALEXANDER (*raises his eyebrows*) Really?

STEPHEN Not actually one person, just a combina-
tion of persons.

ALEXANDER But they're all so . . .

STEPHEN Unsympathetic. I know. But you can't help
liking them, don't you think?

ALEXANDER Unsympathetic is OK. They're just a little,
just a little . . . *passive.*

STEPHEN Passive?

ALEXANDER They don't do anything.

STEPHEN They're miners. They mine.

ALEXANDER For three hundred pages?

STEPHEN Three hundred and fifty. (*with irony*) You
should've seen the first draft.

ALEXANDER (*ignores him*) And the title . . .

STEPHEN What about the title?

ALEXANDER 'Black'.

STEPHEN What's wrong with it?

ALEXANDER	It stinks. (ALEXANDER *notices that* STEPHEN *is looking dejected.*) Look, I tried to like the book, Steve, I really did. After all, I like *you*. But somehow this isn't quite there for me. As I said, I read it again . . .
STEPHEN	(*thinks*) Where?
ALEXANDER	Where what?
STEPHEN	Where did you read it?
ALEXANDER	What does it matter?
STEPHEN	Over breakfast? On the bus? In the shower?
ALEXANDER	Yes, yes.
STEPHEN	What?
ALEXANDER	All those things . . . (*gets up*) Look, I couldn't find anything to . . . anything to get my teeth into. I don't quite know what's wrong with it . . . And it's not just me.
STEPHEN	(*curious*) Who else has read it?
ALEXANDER	Samantha. She read it last week.
STEPHEN	I'm popular. She read it last week, you read it since Tuesday . . . (*laughs*) Don't you guys have anything better to do?
ALEXANDER	(*ignores him*) She has the same problems with it I have.
STEPHEN	Which are?
ALEXANDER	Its . . . elusiveness.
STEPHEN	Elusiveness?
ALEXANDER	One just doesn't know where one stands.
STEPHEN	That was sort of my point.
ALEXANDER	But couldn't something happen? Like . . .
STEPHEN	A tunnel cave in?
ALEXANDER	Maybe that's a little too crass . . .
STEPHEN	Sure.

ALEXANDER I was thinking of something more subtle...
But tragedy should *definitely* strike.

STEPHEN No.

ALEXANDER No?

STEPHEN It's not really that sort of book.

ALEXANDER It could be.

STEPHEN I know it *could* be. (ALEXANDER *looks at him challengingly*) (*resigned*) Maybe it could be.

ALEXANDER Think about it.

STEPHEN But it would take on an entirely different dimension.

ALEXANDER We could work on something like that.

STEPHEN I don't know.

ALEXANDER Think about it, but . . .

STEPHEN But?

ALEXANDER I wish I had those notes. (*He presses the intercom.*) Samantha?
(*When there is no reply,* ALEXANDER *gets up from his desk, opens the door and looks into reception area.*)

STEPHEN She's not there.

ALEXANDER (*closes door*) I can see that.

STEPHEN You've given her the day off.

ALEXANDER I have?

STEPHEN Her sister-in-law's in town. Apparently a big excuse to go shopping.

ALEXANDER I plainly forgot . . . How did you know?

STEPHEN We speak almost every week. She tells me everything.

ALEXANDER (*raises his eyebrows*) Everything?

STEPHEN Everything that doesn't interest me. We've become quite close over the years.

ALEXANDER You have?

STEPHEN Don't you remember?

ALEXANDER What?

STEPHEN How you took me on?

ALEXANDER You wrote in?

STEPHEN Yes.

ALEXANDER So?

STEPHEN I wrote in, and you didn't reply . . .

ALEXANDER Do you have any idea how ma . . .

STEPHEN (*quick*) Eighty in a good week, forty in a bad one. Or surely for an agent it must be the other way round? The more manuscripts that drop through the letterbox, the more you have to deal with. Better if just one drops in a month . . .

ALEXANDER Or none at all . . .

STEPHEN Or none at all. After all you have plenty of chums and celebrities to keep you in fodder for years.

ALEXANDER That's unfair.

STEPHEN Is it? How many good manuscripts do you ever get through the door . . .

ALEXANDER Unsolicited?

STEPHEN I prefer to call them potential masterpieces you never knew existed . . .

ALEXANDER None.

STEPHEN None?

ALEXANDER Ask anyone. Agents. Publishers. Ninety-nine point nine percent of the typescripts that come through the door aren't worth reading.

STEPHEN So one in a thousand is?

ALEXANDER Just a manner of speaking.

STEPHEN So you don't read them?

ALEXANDER Of course we do.

STEPHEN You do?

ALEXANDER We glance at them.

STEPHEN Aren't you afraid that you may miss something?

ALEXANDER We sometimes do. . . . Someone we turned down is making a fortune over at . . .

STEPHEN I mean authors who you just passed over and never hear of again.

ALEXANDER All great writers make it sooner or later . . .

STEPHEN (*laughs*) How can you say that?

ALEXANDER I'm not so sure. Do you really think there are masterpieces that no one has read?

STEPHEN Thousands.

ALEXANDER I wish I could share your optimism.

STEPHEN So where does a writer begin?

ALEXANDER Please, Stephen.

STEPHEN Please, indulge me. I'm genuinely interested. Where does a writer begin?

ALEXANDER If there were no hurdles anything could get published. Where would the quality control be?

STEPHEN With the reader?

ALEXANDER The reader? How do you think they choose what to buy? The press, TV, advertising.

STEPHEN But you're choosing for them, without even reading everything properly. Don't you think that's kind of presumptuous?

ALEXANDER Someone has to.

STEPHEN And why you of all people?

ALEXANDER I like to think I know what people want

to read.

STEPHEN   You *think* or you *know*?

ALEXANDER   No one could be so presumptuous as to know everything. But I'm doing reasonably well, which means . . .

STEPHEN   . . . that you know what *sells*, but do you know what's *good*?

ALEXANDER   And what is the difference?

STEPHEN   Please!

ALEXANDER   I thought there was a distinction once, but now I'm not so sure anymore. (ALEXANDER *gets up*) I'd like to see it as Darwin's theory of evolution. If these hurdles were not in place, the bad writers wouldn't be weeded out.

STEPHEN   Bad writers?

ALEXANDER   Those who don't persevere.

STEPHEN   What has perseverance to do with writing?

ALEXANDER   But is has to.

STEPHEN   But why?

ALEXANDER   If you spend a number of years working on a typescript, don't you think you should make the extra effort to publicise yourself?

STEPHEN   You're talking about two very different sorts of people here.

ALEXANDER   Am I?

STEPHEN   One an intensely private individual, completely unsure about his or her abilities, and the other the exact opposite.

ALEXANDER   It can't be helped. Maybe a hundred years ago people were allowed to come through who didn't have both skills.

STEPHEN   (*gets angry*) Allowed to get through?

Chekhov made it, but for each Chekhov how many others were out there who sent off their typescript and were discouraged by a handful of snotty, offhand responses?

ALEXANDER That's life. Deal with it.

STEPHEN How about the editor who told Fitzgerald that his latest book would be much better without that Gatsby character?

ALEXANDER Everyone likes to quote that.

STEPHEN Because it's true.

ALEXANDER Inevitably there are some casualties.

STEPHEN (*almost angry*) Casualties that people like you could go some way towards preventing!

(ALEXANDER *looks hurt, and* STEPHEN *knows he's gone too far.*)

I'm sorry.

ALEXANDER (*gets up*) That's quite all right.

STEPHEN I don't know what came over me.

ALEXANDER It's OK. Really, it's OK.

STEPHEN It's been a bad week . . . A bad *year*. Nothing's going right for me. This book. I'd do anything to get it published.

ALEXANDER Look . . . (*walks over to the window*) Are you happy?

STEPHEN Happy?

ALEXANDER Yes.

STEPHEN (*shrugs his shoulders*) I guess.

ALEXANDER As I tell all my clients – and I think I told you when I took you on board – I see this as more than just a business relationship. I'd like to see it as a personal one. And I'd like to see that the people with the agency are

	happy.
STEPHEN	That's nice. I'd also like to see it as a . . . personal one.
ALEXANDER	So?
STEPHEN	What?
ALEXANDER	Are you happy. With us? The agency.
STEPHEN	Of course I'm happy.
ALEXANDER	Why?
STEPHEN	You just have to take a look at your list.
ALEXANDER	The list. The list.
STEPHEN	If I'd ever thought I'd be in the company of . . .
ALEXANDER	(*interrupts*) It's not about the *list*. It's about the *people*. So when I'm asking whether you're happy . . .
STEPHEN	I am.
ALEXANDER	. . . it's not just about whether you're happy with the *agency*. I mean, are you happy as a *person*?
STEPHEN	As a person?
ALEXANDER	Exactly.
STEPHEN	(*thinks*) Well . . .
ALEXANDER	Yes?
STEPHEN	I suppose things could be better.
ALEXANDER	I see.
STEPHEN	But they *are* getting better. I sold my first book, just finished the second.
ALEXANDER	It can't be easy.
STEPHEN	Writing?
ALEXANDER	And living on what you're making. A child.
STEPHEN	Two.
ALEXANDER	Two children . . . What do you make a

year? 30, 40k?

STEPHEN   I made ten thousand last year.

ALEXANDER   Writing?

STEPHEN   No, of course not. Doing this and that.

ALEXANDER   What?

STEPHEN   Editing, proof-reading . . . But Clare's working part-time now.

ALEXANDER   She's supportive. That's good. (*thinks*). I know someone who may be interested.

STEPHEN   In the book?

ALEXANDER   No . . . proof-reading.

STEPHEN   No, really, I'd rather . . .

ALEXANDER   No, I'll pass on your name. What with school fees . . .

STEPHEN   (*perplexed*) School fees?

ALEXANDER   I understand that you have to pursue your dream, Steve, who doesn't? But in the meantime why not make some money? Look, good writers don't necessarily get published, just as bad ones necessarily don't. That's life.

STEPHEN   (*ironic*) But isn't that where you should come in? You know, like Robin Hood. Make the world right again?

ALEXANDER   (*genuinely astonished*) Whatever gave you that idea? Writers often forget that this business, like any other, is about money.

STEPHEN   (*laughs nervously*) I don't mind money.

ALEXANDER   In the end you have to decide whether it's worth someone's while to print the damn thing. And make a decent profit out of it. Do you ever think about how many books you'd like to sell?

STEPHEN	A few.
ALEXANDER	Ten-thousand? A hundred-thousand?
STEPHEN	A thousand would be nice, to be honest.
ALEXANDER	A thousand? Where's the profit in that? We all have to make a living.
STEPHEN	And I don't?
ALEXANDER	If I can live from your fifteen percent, imagine how rich you'll be!
STEPHEN	But you have more than one author.
ALEXANDER	That's true. But I can't just put all my eggs in one basket.
STEPHEN	(*thinks*) How many clients do you have?
ALEXANDER	Enough.
STEPHEN	I was only asking. (*insists*) More than thirty. A hundred? . . . A thousand?
ALEXANDER	Don't be ridiculous.
STEPHEN	But more than a hundred?
ALEXANDER	Around that, yes.
STEPHEN	A hundred and twenty?
ALEXANDER	A hundred is fair.
STEPHEN	So, if ten earn a decent living, you'll make a decent living.
ALEXANDER	In theory, yes. But there are overheads.
STEPHEN	And what about the other ninety? The ninety writers who you have on your books, who *don't* make money?
ALEXANDER	That's the nature of the business, I'm afraid. Nothing I can do about it.
STEPHEN	(*visibly upset, but manages to control himself.*) I just can't help thinking that if you spent a little more time . . .
ALEXANDER	Time!
STEPHEN	What do you need to sell a book?

ALEXANDER I have to believe in it.

STEPHEN Believe that it's good?

ALEXANDER No, not necessarily. Believe that something can sell.

STEPHEN And that could apply to anything?

ALEXANDER (*shrugs shoulders*) I guess.

STEPHEN Non-fiction, science-fiction, cookbooks, children's books . . .

ALEXANDER Sure.

STEPHEN . . . as long as you believe that there could be some money in it?

ALEXANDER But I have to *believe* it.

STEPHEN A novel about miners . . .

ALEXANDER I know what you're getting at.

STEPHEN OK: my book. Not the greatest book ever written, but not bad, I'd like to think. Better than a lot of the stuff you get from your chums, maybe. Could you sell it if you genuinely believed it could make money?

ALEXANDER But I don't.

STEPHEN Just suppose.

ALEXANDER You're not being fair.

STEPHEN What if I could convince you that you're wrong? That it will sell.

ALEXANDER Whatever you say, I just don't believe it can work.

STEPHEN But let's assume for a second that you're wrong . . .

ALEXANDER I could well be. As I said, it's a matter of taste. Just because the book isn't for me doesn't mean there isn't a right agent for you out there somewhere.

STEPHEN	I thought . . .
ALEXANDER	It's not for me, as I said. I think you're better off with someone else. Someone . . .
STEPHEN	Hungrier?
ALEXANDER	I was going to say someone who's more up your street. But you could say 'hungrier', if you want to put it like that. (*looks at his watch*) Not that I'm not hungry. I can be pretty hungry if I want to be. (*back to* STEPHEN) Listen, Steve, you need to be with someone who needs to make your books work. You're talented, I told you.
STEPHEN	You don't think I am wasting my time?
ALEXANDER	As a writer?
STEPHEN	Yes.
ALEXANDER	Writing is a strange profession. Look, I'd love to have a chat, but unfortunately . . . (*looks at his watch*) Christ, look at the time! (*presses the intercom*) Paul?
MALE VOICE	(*on intercom*) Yes.
ALEXANDER	Will you order a cab for me and make a reservation for me at the usual?
MALE VOICE	(*on intercom*) What time?
ALEXANDER	(*into intercom*) At twelve. For three people. (*to* STEPHEN) Sorry, something I really can't get out of.
	(ALEXANDER *starts to get ready to go.*)
STEPHEN	Can I ask you a question?
ALEXANDER	Shoot.
STEPHEN	Is it worth me going on? Should I just stop writing and just get myself a normal job . . . ?
ALEXANDER	Are there any normal jobs?

STEPHEN   I need to know. You know, as a writer I get
          two kinds of responses: from friends and
          family, 'Yeah you're great and well done
          and why don't those bastards publish you?'
          And then there's the rest of the world, the
          ones who just shit all over your work, not
          by reading it, you understand, but by
          ignoring it. By not even giving it a fair
          shot. (ALEXANDER *gets up.*) Please, I need
          to know.

ALEXANDER (*takes his briefcase*) I wouldn't have taken
          you on if we didn't think you had some-
          thing.

STEPHEN   Tell me straight. This is really important to
          me. Am I wasting my time?
          (ALEXANDER *looks at* STEPHEN *with pity,*
          puts the case down again and sits down on the
          edge of his desk.)

ALEXANDER Let me tell you a story. One of my col-
          leagues once came to me and told me that
          she had this writer who she'd represented
          for ten, twelve years and she couldn't really
          admit to herself that she hated his books.
          She just *hated* them. Not the first, that was-
          n't bad and it was published to some good
          reviews, and the second made it too, but
          every year he delivered a book to her – no
          chance of writer's block for him – and she
          just grew to hate them and so did every-
          body else she showed them to. Problem
          was he was such a nice guy, she became
          really friendly with him, and his family.
          They even spent the odd Christmas

together. But every spring, like clockwork, the new typescript landed on her desk. Every year it was a little longer, a little heavier, a little more worthy and a little more unpublishable. She dreaded every new book. She asked me what to do.

STEPHEN What did you tell her?

ALEXANDER What would you do?

STEPHEN Fire him?

ALEXANDER After twenty years?

STEPHEN If he was wasting her time?

ALEXANDER And she was wasting his.

STEPHEN Sure. So what did you do?

ALEXANDER We told him that his last book was no good. Sorry. Nothing we can do. Not a chance in hell.

STEPHEN And you fired him.

ALEXANDER No, he quit.

STEPHEN After twenty years?

ALEXANDER Disloyal bastard, eh?

(*They laugh for a second or so.* ALEXANDER *looks at* STEPHEN.)

He signed with another agent and the book hit the jackpot. (*shrugs his shoulders*) So, in answer to your question. Are you wasting your time? No. Am I wasting yours? Yes.

STEPHEN And I'm wasting yours.

ALEXANDER (*kindly*) Let me email you some numbers . . .

STEPHEN But I already said . . .

ALEXANDER . . . of agents you could call.

STEPHEN You're letting me go?

ALEXANDER It's in your own best interest.

STEPHEN Look, I will rewrite it. I think you had a
point. About . . .

ALEXANDER It's not going to work.

STEPHEN How do you know?

ALEXANDER It's my job.

STEPHEN And what *is* your job exactly?

ALEXANDER Stephen.

STEPHEN No, really.

ALEXANDER I'm running late. (*looks at his watch demonstratively*) You know what an agent does.
Now, if you'll excuse me …

STEPHEN No, I don't. I sold my first book myself.
You did the contract.

ALEXANDER And that's nothing?

STEPHEN Not that I didn't appreciate it . . .

ALEXANDER But we did try to sell it overseas.

STEPHEN Did you?

ALEXANDER I can show you the rejections. They're not
pretty.

STEPHEN But you said this one was better.

ALEXANDER It's an improvement.

STEPHEN So what do you do when you sell books?

ALEXANDER You know.

STEPHEN No, I don't know.

ALEXANDER Well, you talk them up. People get excited.
(*looks through some papers*) I don't really
have time for this.

STEPHEN On the phone?

ALEXANDER Yes, on the phone, mostly. But also at
meetings, lunches, parties . . .

STEPHEN Did you ever have lunch and talk about
me?

ALEXANDER Sure.

STEPHEN	When? With whom?
ALEXANDER	I don't know when and with whom. We mention people. That's our job.
STEPHEN	Did you ever talk *me* up?
ALEXANDER	But of course I did. Look . . .
STEPHEN	Show me what an agent does. Give me a practical demonstration.
ALEXANDER	I really don't have time for this.
STEPHEN	Make time.
ALEXANDER	How?
STEPHEN	Pretend I'm your most important writer. Just for today.
ALEXANDER	And why would I want to do that?
STEPHEN	Because . . . (*hesitates*) . . . I have a gun.
ALEXANDER	(*laughs*) A gun?
STEPHEN	In my briefcase.
ALEXANDER	(*curious, but cautious*) Let me see.
STEPHEN	OK.
	(STEPHEN opens his bag and rummages through it. ALEXANDER is beginning to look a little nervous.)
STEPHEN	(*searching*) Not a real gun, of course . . .
ALEXANDER	For a moment I thought . . .
STEPHEN	. . . more of a metaphorical one.
ALEXANDER	I don't follow.
STEPHEN	I'm talking about pictures.
ALEXANDER	Pictures?
STEPHEN	Photographs.
ALEXANDER	Photographs of what?
STEPHEN	Why, of you, of course.
ALEXANDER	(*laughs nervously*) Of me?
STEPHEN	With a certain someone.
ALEXANDER	(*a little relieved*) But she knows about that.

STEPHEN Yes, but does she know *everything*?

ALEXANDER Everything?

STEPHEN Ah, there they are. For minute I thought I left them at the shop. I'm just like you; keep misplacing things. One day I'll misplace one of my manuscripts, but I guess that wouldn't be the end of the world. My wife says that if my head wasn't screwed on . . .

ALEXANDER (*impatient*) Whatever.
(STEPHEN *opens the envelope, flicks through them, almost deliberately slowly.*)

STEPHEN I picked them up this morning. When I have trouble writing, I like to go for walks. With the kids. They go off running and playing and I have some time to think . . .

ALEXANDER I'm waiting.

STEPHEN I just happened to buy a disposable camera. I hadn't taken any pictures on my daughter's birthday . . . I thought it'd be a good idea . . . You just happened to be there . . .

ALEXANDER I don't understand. Be where?

STEPHEN The park. (ALEXANDER *begins to understand.*) It's funny that we should share a park. Our lives are so different. I've a small, terraced house at the bottom of the hill, you must have a two, three bedroom apartment . . .

ALEXANDER Five.

STEPHEN . . . with a nice view. (*flicks through pictures*) Maybe I should've come over, but I didn't want to disturb you. I thought: 'He's busy enough during the week for me to disturb him on a weekend. The last thing he wants to do is bump into a *writer*. On a weekend out with his kids . . . ' But then I realised that you didn't have any kids.

ALEXANDER   I don't.

STEPHEN   And not just one, *two*. I must say they don't half look like you. (*He hands over some pictures one by one to* ALEXANDER.) That's Zoe, my youngest. She's five, it was her birthday last week. That's Kate, she's eight.

ALEXANDER   But . . .

STEPHEN   Sorry. Here's one of you. (*hands him the picture*) At the back, see.

ALEXANDER   But that's hardly . . .

STEPHEN   (*hands him another picture*) That's the best one. Don't you think . . . ? What are their names?

ALEXANDER   I don't get your point.

STEPHEN   The pictures . . . I thought your wife . . .

ALEXANDER   What about Elaine?

STEPHEN   She doesn't know about these two, does she?

ALEXANDER   But of course she does.

STEPHEN   Not the last time I heard.
(ALEXANDER *picks up the phone;*
STEPHEN *suddenly doesn't seem so self-confident any more.*)
What are you doing?

ALEXANDER   Calling her.

STEPHEN   Who?

ALEXANDER   Elaine . . .

STEPHEN   But . . .

ALEXANDER (*indicates for* STEPHEN *to be quiet, into
            receiver*) Hi darling . . . Fine . . . No . . .
            Busy . . . I was just wondering . . . I was
            just wondering . . . I know I shouldn't ask
            you . . . But I'm stuck for an idea of what
            to get the twins for their birthday . . .
            (ALEXANDER *glances up at* STEPHEN *tri-
            umphantly*) No, I don't think so . . . (*the
            intercom buzzes*) Not a bad . . . (*the intercom
            buzzes again*) Not a bad . . . Hang on a sec,
            darling . . . (*into intercom, impatiently*) Yes?!

MALE VOICE (*on intercom*) It's your wife on line one.
            (ALEXANDER *looks at* STEPHEN *crestfallen,
            and puts the receiver down.*)

ALEXANDER (*into intercom*) I'll have to call her back . . .
            And, Paul . . .

MALE VOICE (*on intercom*) Yes?

ALEXANDER (*into intercom*) Please cancel my lunch and
            hold all calls.

MALE VOICE (*on intercom*) But . . .

ALEXANDER (*into intercom*) Just do it, please.
            (*There's a brief silence.*)

STEPHEN What are their names?

ALEXANDER (*resigned*) Max and Andrew.

STEPHEN Agents' names.

ALEXANDER What do you mean?

STEPHEN Do you think they'll be agents when they
          grow up? Or writers like their mother?

ALEXANDER That's none of your business.

STEPHEN She's got the kind of face that sells.

ALEXANDER She's a great writer.

STEPHEN Something like a self-fulfilling prophecy.
          You decide someone's a great writer and,

oops, they are.

ALEXANDER   I think you're overestimating an agent's power.

STEPHEN   You're not just an agent. You're *the* agent.

ALEXANDER   We're just part of the process.

STEPHEN   More like a bridge. And most writers can't swim.

ALEXANDER   (*impatient*) The pictures.

STEPHEN   The pictures. Yes. I don't know why I took them. I certainly didn't think they'd come in handy . . . so soon.

ALEXANDER   Give them to me.

STEPHEN   Here. (*he hands him the rest of the photographs.*)

ALEXANDER   The *negatives*.

STEPHEN   No.

ALEXANDER   What do you want?

STEPHEN   (*teases*) What have you got?

ALEXANDER   If you're looking for cash . . .

STEPHEN   I don't want your money.
(ALEXANDER *buries his head in his hands.*)

ALEXANDER   I meant to tell her, really I did . . .

STEPHEN   '. . . but there never was a right time'.

ALEXANDER   I hadn't seen the twins for a year. She wanted to meet to discuss things, she insisted on the park. I knew it was a mistake. (*buries his head in his hands*) You must know what it's like . . .

STEPHEN   No, I don't.

ALEXANDER   The constant parties, the flirting, the long hours . . . Soon you can't tell real affection from flirtation any more. When she became pregnant, what could I do? . . .

STEPHEN   You could have stopped being a hypocrite.

ALEXANDER   (*looks up at* STEPHEN) Elaine can't have children. She said she didn't want children anyway. I pretended to be fine with it, I *was* fine with it, but when . . . (*he can't carry on.*)

STEPHEN   I see.

(STEPHEN *almost looks sorry.*)

ALEXANDER   If she ever found out it would kill her. Please give me the negatives. Give them to me and we'll forget all about it.

STEPHEN   (*with only the slightest hesitation*) No.

ALEXANDER   What do you want?

STEPHEN   I've just come to get what by rights should be mine anyway.

ALEXANDER   Which is?

STEPHEN   An agent.

ALEXANDER   Look, all right. We'll give it another try. We give ourselves a couple of months and if no one bites, we think again. Why don't you leave it with me . . . ?

STEPHEN   No.

ALEXANDER   In this business you have to be patient.

STEPHEN   I'm all out of patience.

ALEXANDER   Stephen, with the best will in the world, there's nothing I can do about it.

STEPHEN   Are you sure?

ALEXANDER   Positive.

STEPHEN   And you really expect me to believe that?

(STEPHEN *looks at* ALEXANDER *challengingly,* ALEXANDER *turns away.*)

I think we should have an auction.

ALEXANDER Auction?

STEPHEN You know what an auction is. We auction the book. The highest bidder gets it.

ALEXANDER (*laughs in disbelief*) We can't just auction a book. Especially not this book.

STEPHEN Why not?

ALEXANDER Well, for a start it's . . .

STEPHEN Boring?

ALEXANDER You yourself want to rewrite it.

STEPHEN I don't.

ALEXANDER But you said . . .

STEPHEN I lied. To humour you. I'm happy with the book, *very* happy. I wouldn't change a word.

ALEXANDER I can see you're upset. Look, let's try it this way. I'll send it out to a couple of publishers and we'll see what they say. But for God's sake, let's all be grown-ups here. Let's talk about this.

STEPHEN Isn't that what we've been doing? Talking? Now talk to someone else.

ALEXANDER You're crazy.

STEPHEN Get some of your publishers on the phone. Tell them, tell them … Tell them whatever you say when you talk things up. (*paces up and down while thinking*) Tell them you've come across a great book, a once-in-a-lifetime thing, written by a newcomer. First novel, magnificent. Tell them it's by a woman, a young woman, a young, *attractive* woman. Tell them she'll look good on TV.

ALEXANDER What, *lie*? (STEPHEN *laughs*.) I don't want

to do this.

STEPHEN   I know. (*indicates the envelope with the nega-tives*) What do you think I need these for?

ALEXANDER   This is ridiculous. Give them to me.
(ALEXANDER *slowly starts to get up and wants to approach* STEPHEN.)

STEPHEN   You really think you can get these off me?

ALEXANDER   Give them to me.

STEPHEN   No.
(ALEXANDER *tries to grab the pictures, but* STEPHEN *pushes him away easily. It's evident that he wouldn't stand a chance.*)
(*Reluctantly* ALEXANDER *steps back and sits down again.*)

ALEXANDER   All right. Who do you want me to call?

STEPHEN   Five publishers. The big five. The ones with money.

ALEXANDER   You know you're not going to get away with it.

STEPHEN   Let *me* worry about that. Dial. (ALEXANDER reluctantly *picks up the phone.*)
Speakerphone.
(ALEXANDER *puts the receiver down again, and presses the speakerphone button. We hear a dial tone and he presses a button and the phone speed-dials.*)
(*The phone is answered.*)

CHARLIE   (*on speakerphone*) Hello? (ALEXANDER *looks at* STEPHEN *once again, but* STEPHEN *signals him to carry on.*) (CHARLIE *on speakerphone*) Hello?

ALEXANDER   Charlie?

CHARLIE   (*on speakerphone*) Alex, how are you? Are

	you still on for tomorrow night?
ALEXANDER	If you're buying.
CHARLIE	(*on speakerphone*) You know things are tight around here.
ALEXANDER	Not from what I've been hearing. One mil for that turkey? You should get some of our guys. Twice the money but four times the profit.
CHARLIE	(*on speakerphone*) Never. What can I do for you?
ALEXANDER	Read a book.
CHARLIE	(*on speakerphone*) If you're still waiting for that thing, I had it back from the reader yesterday and it doesn't look good.
ALEXANDER	I'm not talking about that. I have something hot for you.
CHARLIE	(*on speakerphone*) You always have something hot.
ALEXANDER	This is different. This is *real* hot.
CHARLIE	(*on speakerphone*) What's it about?
ALEXANDER	It's about to make you rich.
CHARLIE	(*on speakerphone*) Where have I heard that one before?
ALEXANDER	You don't want to miss out on this one. New author. First book . . .
CHARLIE	(*on speakerphone, groans*) Not another great first novel!
ALEXANDER	. . . great looking . . .
CHARLIE	(*on speakerphone*) Woman?
ALEXANDER	Of course a woman.
CHARLIE	(*on speakerphone*) What's it called?
ALEXANDER	(*looks at* STEPHEN) 'Black'.
CHARLIE	(*on speakerphone*) Title stinks.

ALEXANDER   (*looks at* STEPHEN, *indicating 'I told you so'*) As I said, you've got to read it.

CHARLIE   (*on speakerphone*) Send it on over. I'll get someone to have a look at it over the weekend.

ALEXANDER   (*hesitates, glances at* STEPHEN) I'm going to auction it.

CHARLIE   (*on speakerphone*) You're kidding.

ALEXANDER   No.

CHARLIE   (*on speakerphone*) That good, huh?

ALEXANDER   This writer is . . . *special*.

CHARLIE   (*on speakerphone*) Don't do this to me. I've got too much . . .

ALEXANDER   It's hot.

CHARLIE   (on speakerphone, sceptical) First-time author?

ALEXANDER   Trust me on this.

CHARLIE   (*on speakerphone*) OK, I'll take a look at it. But if it's shit . . .

ALEXANDER   I know, I know.

CHARLIE   (*on speakerphone*) Listen, I have to go. When do you want me to get back to you? (ALEXANDER *looks at* STEPHEN, *who briefly considers, then raises three fingers.*)

ALEXANDER   Three o'clock.

CHARLIE   (*on speakerphone, astonished*) Today?

ALEXANDER   It's got to be done now . . . It's worth it.

CHARLIE   (*on speakerphone*) It better be.

ALEXANDER   I'll email it over to you. Call me on my private number. Speak to you at three.

CHARLIE   (*on speakerphone*) Don't count on it. (CHARLIE *puts the phone down*, ALEXAN-DER *presses the speakerphone button to discon-*

nect.)

ALEXANDER   Happy?

STEPHEN   Not bad . . . Next.

(ALEXANDER *sighs and prepares to dial another number.*)

(*As we hear the dial tone, the lights fade*).

ACT II

A few hours have passed. The bright morning sunlight has been replaced by the more sombre light of a hazy afternoon. The hands of the clock on the wall are approaching 3 o'clock.

On ALEXANDER's *desk are a few cartons that contain expensive Chinese take-away food.*

STEPHEN *is standing at a bookshelf, looking at a book, but can't concentrate and starts pacing up and down.*

ALEXANDER *is sitting at his desk, eating from one of the cartons with chopsticks.*

ALEXANDER   Sure you don't want some? (STEPHEN *ignores him.*) It's delicious.

STEPHEN   No, thank you.

ALEXANDER   Your loss.

   (ALEXANDER *takes another bite, looks at* STEPHEN, *who is still pacing up and down.*)

ALEXANDER   At least sit down. You're making me nervous.

STEPHEN   *I'm* making *you* nervous?

ALEXANDER   Sit down. Have something.

STEPHEN   Like what?

ALEXANDER   A cigarette?

STEPHEN   I don't smoke.

ALEXANDER   I'd offer you a drink but I'm on the

wagon.

(STEPHEN *sits down reluctantly, looks up at the clock, taps his feet restlessly*.)

STEPHEN Shouldn't you call them and find out what they thought?

ALEXANDER I know what I'm doing.

STEPHEN I don't know how you can eat.

(ALEXANDER *contemplates* STEPHEN's *food, looks up at him*.)

Go ahead.

(ALEXANDER *helps himself to* STEPHEN's *portion*.)

ALEXANDER This is my favourite part.

STEPHEN What?

ALEXANDER Waiting.

STEPHEN You must be kidding.

ALEXANDER Who wants to go fishing when you can do this? And get paid for it. (*takes another bite*) You know what the best part about being an agent is?

STEPHEN The money?

ALEXANDER There's that, of course.

STEPHEN The parties, the schmoozing?

ALEXANDER Nope.

STEPHEN (*impatient*) What then?

ALEXANDER The deal. It's like an addiction. You just can't get enough. The book's the first step, of course, but once it's gone out of the door the deal is all that matters. I just love waiting while they're trying to figure out what I want.

STEPHEN I seem to spend my whole life waiting.

ALEXANDER (*checks the clock*) Well, you don't have to

wait much longer. It's almost three.

(STEPHEN *also looks up at the clock, double checks with his wristwatch.*)

STEPHEN   Maybe we should have given them more time.

ALEXANDER   Nonsense.

STEPHEN   What if no one wants it?

ALEXANDER   Only a fool would auction something no one wants. (*takes a bite, remembers*) Of course, this is different.

STEPHEN   The book's boring. No plot, passive characters . . .

ALEXANDER   Who cares?

STEPHEN   How about the people who're reading it? Right now.

ALEXANDER   No one reads these things.

STEPHEN   They don't?

ALEXANDER   Of course they *read* them, but not for what they are. There are no real readers out there anymore. People read to write, or they read to buy, or read to sell . . . Did you know that there are more books on writing than there are on any other subject? No one reads just for the sake of it. (*looks up at* STEPHEN) When was the last time you read a good book? Just for the pleasure of reading?

STEPHEN   Last week.

ALEXANDER   Maybe you're a bad example.

(STEPHEN *gets up again nervously, and stops to look out of the window, but quickly gets bored.*)

(*cautiously*) What are you going to do if

there are no offers?

STEPHEN   But . . .

ALEXANDER   Just supposing the old Alexander magic doesn't work this time.

STEPHEN   Then we have to think of something else.

ALEXANDER   Once an auction fails . . .

STEPHEN   There are other publishers.

ALEXANDER   Small publishers. Low advances. Anything apart from the big five is vanity publishing.

STEPHEN   Vanity *agenting* perhaps. Think of my share. (STEPHEN *stops pacing and looks at* ALEXANDER.)

Don't you want to check the line?

ALEXANDER   It's fine.

STEPHEN   Are you sure?

(ALEXANDER *demonstratively presses the speaker button; a loud dial tone can be heard.*)

ALEXANDER   Satisfied? (ALEXANDER *replaces the phone in the cradle.*)

STEPHEN   What if they just called? You're engaged.

ALEXANDER   They'll call back.

STEPHEN   What if they call the switchboard and they won't be put through?

ALEXANDER   They know who to put through. (*notices* STEPHEN *standing*) Sit down. Relax. (STEPHEN *sits down. There's an awkward pause.*)

STEPHEN   Have you ever been blackmailed before?

ALEXANDER   No, this is my first time.

STEPHEN   Mine too.

ALEXANDER   Glad to hear it. (*Pause.*) I never figured you for the blackmailing type.

STEPHEN   I don't know what got into me.

ALEXANDER   (*shrugs his shoulders*) You thought the book was worth something. That's an excusable mistake. But really writers are in the worst position to judge what they've written, don't you think?

STEPHEN   I just had a good feeling about this one. I thought this was it . . . I was just too bloody confident. I should have listened to you.

ALEXANDER   Maybe the next one will be the one for you.
(STEPHEN *ignores him and starts to pace again*.)

STEPHEN   If this one doesn't work I really don't know what to do. I don't know whether I can go through all this again.

ALEXANDER   Blackmailing or writing a mediocre book?
(STEPHEN *stops, looks at* ALEXANDER *sadly*.) I'm sorry. I didn't mean it like that.

STEPHEN   No, you're right. The last thing the world needs is another writer. (STEPHEN *starts to pace again*) What if it's true that most people have only one book in them? Maybe my first one was my last.

ALEXANDER   Then you *are* in trouble.
(STEPHEN *looks at* ALEXANDER *irritated, and* STEPHEN *starts pacing again*.)

ALEXANDER   You'll write again.

STEPHEN   How do you know?

ALEXANDER   What else would you do? (ALEXANDER *picks up the photographs, flicks through them briefly, puts them away again*.) In a way I admire you. It takes guts to do what you're

doing. Most writers would have walked
away without a fight.

STEPHEN And much good did it do me. I'm waiting
for the phone to ring like a lovesick
teenager.

ALEXANDER If a writer doesn't believe in what he's
writing, why should his agent? But still . . .

STEPHEN I went a little too far.

ALEXANDER You can say that again. (*he contemplates the
envelope in* STEPHEN's *hand.*) Why don't
you give them to me?

STEPHEN I don't know.

ALEXANDER The phone's not ringing.

STEPHEN But you said . . .

ALEXANDER There are no guarantees in this business.
All I could do for you is to get people to
take it seriously. The rest is up to you. (*he
has walked close enough to touch him.*) Give
me the pictures. Please. (STEPHEN *hesitates.*)
Give them to me. You walk on out of here,
and this whole thing is between us.

STEPHEN I don't know.

ALEXANDER I'll still give you the numbers. Minus those
of agents who lead double lives.
(STEPHEN *thinks about it.* ALEXANDER
approaches him slowly and carefully.)
Give me the negatives.

STEPHEN *thinks about it, is about to hand
over the pictures, hesitates.*

The phone rings.

ALEXANDER *glances at the telephone, but doesn't move.*

ALEXANDER   Give them to me.

STEPHEN   Answer it.

ALEXANDER   First the negs.

STEPHEN   (*shouts*) Answer it!

ALEXANDER *walks across to his desk, sits down angrily.*
STEPHEN *looks on anxiously as* ALEXANDER *picks up the phone.*

ALEXANDER   (*into phone*) Yep. (STEPHEN *looks on nervously.*) Yes . . . No . . . I understand . . . No problem . . . (ALEXANDER *puts the phone down.* STEPHEN *looks dejected.*)

STEPHEN   No?

ALEXANDER   Sam's taking tomorrow off as well.
(STEPHEN *lets out a short, bitter laugh and sits down in silence, disappointed.*)

ALEXANDER   You know, when you asked me earlier whether you should go on writing? Would you really have stopped if I'd told you to?

STEPHEN   No.

ALEXANDER   My opinion means nothing to you?

STEPHEN   *Everyone's* opinion means something to me. When someone tells me my writing is shit I believe it, and when someone tells me I'm a genius, I'm fool enough to believe that too. That is until the next opinion comes along. (*he looks at the clock on the wall, double-checks with his wristwatch*)

They're taking their time.

ALEXANDER You'll get your break. Maybe not today,
but you'll get it.

STEPHEN I thought I *had* a break. I sold my first
book. I thought, 'This is it, I'm a writer, I
don't have to be ashamed when people ask
me what I do. I'm a writer.' Do you know
how pretentious that sounds?

ALEXANDER It doesn't sound pretentious at all.

STEPHEN It does to someone who's dreamed of
writing all his life.

ALEXANDER There are bad writers and good writers,
what's the big deal? What's wrong with
calling yourself a writer?

STEPHEN An unpublished writer is nothing.

ALEXANDER Lots of writers were only published
posthumously.

STEPHEN And whose fault is that?

ALEXANDER (*ignores* STEPHEN's *remark*) I don't understand you writers sometimes. Why put
yourselves in that position? Why don't you
stop?

STEPHEN Writing is not a job you *want* to do, it's a
job you *have* to do. Don't you think I wish
I could just do a job like everyone else?
Go to work at nine, be back by six, leave
all my problems at work, get a regular pay
cheque at the end of the month? Just stop?
God knows, I tried. I tried several times.
Thought I'd be happy without a story in
my head. But suddenly you have this idea
and before you know it you're sitting
somewhere making notes. And of course

you always think it could be different this time. You think it'll write itself, that it all falls into place like a dream, but of course it's always more difficult. What you first think will take a couple of months turns into a couple of years. And the terrible thing is that you don't know until right at the end whether it will all fall into place. It's the last few days of writing I enjoy, when you know what you've got, not the months and years that lead up to it. It's all an enormous gamble.

ALEXANDER   Have you ever abandoned a book?

STEPHEN   You never abandon books, they abandon you. At some stage you discover that you're just not the right person to write it. That you've misjudged yourself. The book still exists, but someone else will have to write it. And, invariably, they do.

ALEXANDER   But when you're finished, surely it must all have been worth it?

STEPHEN   Yes, maybe those days are the best. The days between finishing something and before you get the first reader's comments. Good or bad. For those few days every-thing seems possible.

ALEXANDER   Yes . . .

STEPHEN   When it's finished you celebrate, quietly. You send it off to your agent, if you're lucky enough to have one, and start wait-ing. For a few hours, days even, you allow yourself the dream that he'll love it, invite you to lunch, promise you the earth and tell you that all the publishers will come and beat your door down to get their hands on it. But the reality of it always turns out to be the same, at least for me.

You send off the manuscript, and then you wait. You don't hear anything over the next few days – of course he won't read it immediately, after all you're not Ian McEwan – but then a week goes by, then another and doubt sets in. 'He hates it', you think. 'He hates every line of it. Your characters are boring, one-dimensional', you can't bear thinking about it.

When you've waited for a couple of weeks and you can't stand it any longer you dig out the manuscript for the first time since you stuffed a copy into an envelope. You read a couple of paragraphs, as much as you can bear. And it all stares out at you: clumsy sentences, embarrassing story lines, but nothing is as bad as realising your overall audacity in wanting to be a writer in the first place.

You see your worst fears confirmed, not by your agent, but by yourself. You put the manuscript away again and try to forget about it. And then . . .

(STEPHEN *pauses, notices that* ALEXANDER *is hooked.*)

ALEXANDER What?

STEPHEN Nothing. For another few weeks. You send a few emails. Nothing. Then you muster your courage and phone up. He's 'in a

meeting', he's 'busy'. Not with your stuff,
you assume, with other, more important
writers; those who have no problems writing, no problems delivering, those with
tons of self-confidence who don't need
anyone to tell them they're any good.

ALEXANDER No such thing.

STEPHEN And you finally get to know the assistant
well enough . . .

ALEXANDER Samantha.

STEPHEN Samantha, Sarah, Fiona, whatever their
name is. I know them all. You ring them
and they take pity on you and have a word
with him on your behalf. After a few days
she rings back. 'No, he hasn't had time to
read it yet, he's ever so sorry, he'll try to
get round to it this weekend, it's on his
desk, in his briefcase, next to his bed, taped
to the wall of his shower' . . .

ALEXANDER I have so much to read . . .

STEPHEN You know, I never figured it out: why do
agents always read in their spare time? Why
don't they read in the office? It's their job.
There you have the dream job, to read and
discover new talent, and you just regard it
as a hassle . . .

(ALEXANDER *doesn't reply*)

So, he hasn't read it. Fair enough, you're
not his most important client, not even a
semi-important one. But you still had an
arrangement, you thought. You write, he
sells. But instead of being angry with him
for not having read the novel, you're curi-

ously encouraged. He's busy, but he will get round to it, sit down and read it, and he'll get so excited that after a few chapters he'll call. Sure it won't be perfect – whatever is? – but it's not beyond repair.

You dare sneak a look at the manuscript again and all of a sudden it doesn't look too bad. The few typos and handful of clumsy sentences are forgivable – after all you were in a rush to get the baby delivered – but it's all there the way you intended. The theme, the characters, it all comes to life . . . And then . . . then you feel almost satisfied. 'Yes, maybe I'm not so bad after all. Maybe I can call myself a writer.' And then you wait again.
(STEPHEN *relishes* ALEXANDER's *attention, leans forward*) And then . . .

ALEXANDER (*relieved*) . . . I call you.

STEPHEN No.

ALEXANDER No?

STEPHEN No. (*leans back*) I still hear nothing. I send another couple of e-mails, leave a couple of messages. No response. I almost give up, but then, out of the blue, you call me.

ALEXANDER Finally! (*curious*) And what do I say?

STEPHEN What *can* you say? You're all apologetic, of course. Turn on the charm. Things have been hectic, but you were finally able to take out an hour and had a chance to read it. At the end of the conversation I feel amazed that I have such a wonderful agent, someone who actually takes the time to

read my stuff. You ask me to come for a
meeting. I'm so flattered to get a call from
you at all, that when I put the phone
down, I realise that you haven't said what
you think.

ALEXANDER Yes.

STEPHEN And here we are.

ALEXANDER And here we are.

STEPHEN And no one is calling. (STEPHEN *looks up
at the clock, which now shows several minutes
after three o'clock.*) I guess that's it.

ALEXANDER People never meet deadlines. As a writer
you should know that.

STEPHEN You were right, I was wrong. The book's
nonsense.

ALEXANDER Trust me . . . They're playing with me.

STEPHEN I wouldn't be so sure.

ALEXANDER (*leans back*) I bet they've started doing the
figures after reading a few chapters. 'Let
him think we don't want it, but we do
want it, want it badly. Let him think we've
forgotten the time. But this book is hot.'

STEPHEN Are we still talking about the same book?

ALEXANDER It's not the book anymore.

STEPHEN Then what am I doing here?
(STEPHEN *grabs his bag and gets up.*)

ALEXANDER Where do you think you're going?

STEPHEN Let's just forget about it.
(ALEXANDER *gets up.*)

ALEXANDER You can't do that.

STEPHEN Why? I thought you'd be happy. You're off
the hook.

ALEXANDER Don't you get it? This is not about you any

49

more.

STEPHEN   It isn't?

ALEXANDER   It's me who's on the line here; not you, *me*.
            What do you think my 'chums' will do to
            me if they find out about this?

STEPHEN   That's your problem. I'm out of here.

ALEXANDER   Like it or not, we're in it together now. I
            have my reputation to protect.

STEPHEN   And I don't?

ALEXANDER   I think it's a little late to worry about your
            reputation.
            (STEPHEN *heads for the door.*)
            Do you think this is the first novel I dislike
            that I'm stuck with? (STEPHEN *stops.*) This
            is the first time I've been blackmailed in
            the traditional sense, sure, but do you think
            I can really pick and choose what I want
            to represent? What you call the laziness of
            representing my chums is just part of the
            system. Sure you peddle a lot of rubbish,
            things that are far worse than your novel –
            believe me – and which fetch far more
            than you'll make in a lifetime. But to get
            the cream you have to deal with a certain
            amount of . . . froth. But what's the harm if
            it sells?

STEPHEN   Do you really think there's still a chance?

ALEXANDER   I honestly don't know. I honestly don't
            know. (STEPHEN *hesitates.*) We've gone
            this far; let's just see what happens.

STEPHEN   Why?

ALEXANDER   Just call it curiosity. And a certain amount
            of professional pride.

(*Reluctantly* STEPHEN *puts his bag down again and sits down.*)

ALEXANDER Maybe we're not that different. We want the same things, we just have different motives.

STEPHEN Why don't they call?

ALEXANDER They'll call. Even if they pass. Relax.

(STEPHEN *is still holding the pictures in his hand, but they seem to have become meaningless to him.*)

What are you going to do if they pass?

STEPHEN I don't know. Pack it all in, I guess.

ALEXANDER I mean with the pictures.

STEPHEN Maybe I should do you all a favour and send them to her anyway.

(ALEXANDER *looks worried,* STEPHEN *notices.*)

No, *you* have the negatives. You can call the police.

ALEXANDER No need for that. Just the negatives.

STEPHEN At least in prison I'll have time to write.

ALEXANDER They don't give you pen and paper.

STEPHEN That was in the old days. I checked . . .

ALEXANDER You did? Why?

STEPHEN Just in case. A writer's worst nightmare. Being stuck somewhere without something to write.

ALEXANDER I thought it would be quite liberating.

STEPHEN Like being stuck at the bottom of the ocean without oxygen.

(ALEXANDER *gets up.*)

ALEXANDER You writers, you really kill me. Everybody

wants something from me. Everyone thinks I can work magic. 'Just get signed with Alexander, he'll get you published, get you big advances', but it's not as simple as that. In the end it's you who have to take responsibility.

STEPHEN So, where does a self-respecting writer start?

ALEXANDER But I did sign you, didn't I?

STEPHEN You did, and I celebrated. Quietly, because it was only a hurdle. A big hurdle, but I am a realist.

ALEXANDER So I *do* sign people who just write in. (*thinks, more to himself*) Must have been out of my mind.

STEPHEN You didn't.

ALEXANDER But I thought . . .

STEPHEN I heard nothing for months, so I decided to pull a few strings . . . Turned out that Clare's father knows your wife.

ALEXANDER (*laughs*) I am disappointed.

STEPHEN I wasn't proud of it. But I thought, why not? Everybody else uses connections. Finally I could concentrate on writing while someone else takes care of my career. Boy, was I wrong.

ALEXANDER I never promised you any miracles.

STEPHEN No, you didn't. You're not a fool. But I expected more of you than just to send my book to ten of your chums with a luke-warm recommendation and then hope that one of them hits. All you're doing is col-lecting rejections. That much I can do myself. (*thinks*) Being an agent must be like playing the lottery, just with better odds.

ALEXANDER   What do you mean?

STEPHEN   Take a handful of writers. Most have had something published already, probably with some moderate success. The small agencies can take care of that. Just pick the best of the crop after they've proven their worth. Send out their manuscripts, hope that a handful of them sells, screw the others. Get some new ones on board every once in a while to make it look as if you're looking for new talent.

ALEXANDER   But we are.

STEPHEN   No. You *create* the 'talent' by choosing new writers. Just walk into any bookshop and look at the monster you've created.

ALEXANDER   So?

STEPHEN   Don't you feel responsible?

ALEXANDER   The truth is, I don't give a shit. I've had it up to here with baby-sitting broken egos, aspiring egos, or plain pains in the arse. The simple truth is that some books sell, others don't. And if someone chooses to be a writer so be it. It'll be on their head. But don't expect me to be their baby sitter. I'm here to help writers sell their stuff, and it's true, sometimes you need to flatter their ego, but when it comes down to it I'd much rather have a businesslike approach to it. Divide books into two piles: one, short one, of books that sell, and all the bad books, the mediocre books, and even the good books that only have a chance of selling a couple of hundred copies in the other . . .

STEPHEN . . . much larger . . .

ALEXANDER . . . enormous pile. Yes.

(STEPHEN *smiles.*)

ALEXANDER Why are you smiling?

STEPHEN And I thought *I* had problems.

ALEXANDER What?

STEPHEN At least I enjoy what I'm doing. You . . . you don't even like what you're dealing in.

ALEXANDER But I enjoy the deal.

STEPHEN But why deal in books?

ALEXANDER Why not?

STEPHEN Because you can't write?

(ALEXANDER'S *expression suggests that* STEPHEN *has hit the nail on the head.*)

I'm sorry.

ALEXANDER That's OK.

STEPHEN Because you have no time? Because . . .

ALEXANDER Because I *can't*. God knows I tried. My father was a writer. Did I ever tell you that?

STEPHEN No.

ALEXANDER He drank himself to death. Left five novels behind, completely finished. Neatly bound, just as if he was about to send them off to publishers. But he never did send them.

STEPHEN What happened to them?

ALEXANDER No one dared look at them. They were off limits. They were stored in the attic for years. But one day I did. Read them.

STEPHEN   And?

ALEXANDER   What?

STEPHEN   What were they like?

ALEXANDER   Not great, not great at all.

STEPHEN   That must have been disappointing.

ALEXANDER   Not at all. On the contrary: it was oddly
reassuring. I'd always looked up to the old
man; thought I'd never be like him. But
when I found out that he was just as falli-
ble as the rest of us, I felt strangely encouraged.

STEPHEN   (*laughs*) To become an agent?

ALEXANDER   First I wanted to become a writer, of
course. I studied English, found it came
easy to me. After Oxford I took a year off,
went to the South of France to live a little
and write my great first novel. Only it
wouldn't come . . .

STEPHEN   You didn't write anything?

ALEXANDER   Sure I wrote. Nothing could stop me.
Reams of the stuff. I lived the classic life of
a writer in the South of France. The alco-
hol, the drugs, the women . . .

STEPHEN   Women?

ALEXANDER   We're talking Bukowski here, not
Chekhov. But . . .

STEPHEN   But?

ALEXANDER   One day I sobered up, took the opus I'd
produced that summer, and had a good
read.

STEPHEN   And?

ALEXANDER   You know how difficult it is to judge your
own stuff . . .

STEPHEN   Sure.

ALEXANDER   In my case there was no such problem . . .
               It was shit.

STEPHEN   Are you sure?

ALEXANDER   One hundred percent.

STEPHEN   I'm sorry.

ALEXANDER   Don't be. I think that was the best thing
               that could ever happen to me. The greatest
               thing in life is to know the limitation of
               your talents.
               (ALEXANDER *has taken the photographs
               again, and slowly flicks through them one by
               one.*)
               You know, maybe I should tell her. I'm
               tired of living two lives. I think we'd be
               able to survive. What do you think?

STEPHEN   That's for you to decide.

ALEXANDER   I know.
               (*The phone rings.*
               STEPHEN *and* ALEXANDER *look at each
               other.* ALEXANDER *picks up the phone.*)

ALEXANDER   (*on phone*) Yep . . . Let me put you on hold,
               I'm on the other line.
               (ALEXANDER *presses a button.*)

STEPHEN   Who is it?
               (ALEXANDER *looks at* STEPHEN *enigmatical-
               ly, waits a few seconds, presses the button
               again.*)

ALEXANDER   (*on phone*) Hi, Charlie. Nice to hear from
               you. Do you know what time it is?
               (*winks at* STEPHEN) No . . . No? . . .
               (STEPHEN *looks increasingly nervous*) You
               don't think . . . Well, I thought you weren't

right for it . . . I don't know . . . (STEPHEN *gets up, grabs his bag and jacket and heads for the door.*) Sure . . . Get back to me if you change your mind . . . (ALEXANDER *notices* STEPHEN *leaving, indicates for him to stay.*) Thanks for calling . . . Talk to you later. (ALEXANDER *puts the phone down, goes after* STEPHEN.)

Where do you think you're going now?

STEPHEN   I've heard enough.

ALEXANDER   I don't think so.

STEPHEN   What?

ALEXANDER   They just offered twenty-five grand.

STEPHEN   What?

ALEXANDER   UK and Commonwealth.

STEPHEN   (*incredulous, but ecstatic*) What?!

ALEXANDER   Yep.

STEPHEN   But I thought . . .

ALEXANDER   Yes, a pittance. I turned him down.

STEPHEN   You did what?

ALEXANDER   Trust me.

STEPHEN   You turned them down?!

ALEXANDER   If someone wants to pay twenty-five, they'll pay thirty.

STEPHEN   And if they pay thirty . . .

ALEXANDER   . . . they'll pay thirty-five. Exactly.

STEPHEN   What if . . .

ALEXANDER   Sit down. Let me handle this. Am I your agent or not?

(STEPHEN *sits down. As soon as he's put his bag on the floor again, the phone rings again.*)
(*on phone*) Yep . . . Sure . . . OK . . . Get back to you.

(ALEXANDER puts the phone down quickly and rubs his hands in glee.)
We're in business.

STEPHEN   What?

ALEXANDER   Forty.

STEPHEN   Forty?

ALEXANDER   That's only the beginning.

STEPHEN   What?

ALEXANDER   We haven't even started yet.

STEPHEN   (*looks at the clock*) But . . .

ALEXANDER   They're playing it cool.

STEPHEN   What if that's the best offer?

ALEXANDER   It's not.

STEPHEN   Forty thousand is a lot of money.

ALEXANDER   It's worth more.

STEPHEN   But this morning you said . . .

ALEXANDER   Water under the bridge. The book's out
there now and has taken on a life of its
own. This thing could be hot. (*the phone
rings*) And we haven't even talked film
rights yet. (*picks up the phone*) Yep . . . Yep . . .
OK . . . Get back to you. (*puts down the
phone.*)

STEPHEN   Who was that?

ALEXANDER   100k.

STEPHEN   You're kidding.

ALEXANDER   Do I look like I'm kidding?

STEPHEN   Plus . . .

ALEXANDER   Plus the film rights you don't care about.
(ALEXANDER *gets up and starts pacing up
and down the room.*)
I love this, don't you? How do you feel?

STEPHEN   I'm not sure.

(ALEXANDER stops.)

ALEXANDER   What do you mean you're not sure? This is it, don't you realise? You've arrived.

STEPHEN   I feel like an impostor.

ALEXANDER   What?

STEPHEN   Don't these people know I can't write?

ALEXANDER   I don't get you. One moment you're unpublished and think you're a fucking genius, now you have half the publishing world eating out of your hand and you think you're a hack.

STEPHEN   It's just so unexpected.

ALEXANDER   I thought that's what you were dreaming of.

STEPHEN   Dreaming sure, but I am a realist at heart.

ALEXANDER   Steve, cheer up. What are you going to do?

STEPHEN   What?

ALEXANDER   With the money?

STEPHEN   Write. (STEPHEN *looks happy*)
Don't you see? I can finally do what I wanted to do. Write.

ALEXANDER   That's it?

STEPHEN   Sure. Pay off my debts, quit my three day-jobs. Just . . . write.

ALEXANDER   Write?

STEPHEN   I have everything I want.
(*The phone rings.*)

ALEXANDER   Then let me get you some more. (*picks up phone*) Yep . . . OK . . . Can you hold? . . . (*presses a button*) Hi Charlie. No, no can do . . . I'm looking for something a tad higher . . . Sure . . . Sure, there are plenty more books in the pipeline . . . Saw an outline. . .

Not bad . . . Not bad at all . . . Yes . . .
I may be able to live with that . . . Hold
on. (*presses a button*) Sorry . . . No . . . You
have to up the guarantee . . . Paperback . . .
Are you kidding? . . . Let me put you on
hold . . . Let me put you on hold . . . (*presses a button*) Hi . . . A little late, aren't you?
. . . OK . . . I'm always happy to talk . . .
OK . . . Get back to you . . . Promise . . .
(*presses a button*) Give me a figure, Charlie
. . . Are you sure? . . . OK . . . Hold . . .
(*presses a button*) Is that your final offer? . . .
OK . . . Call you back, promise . . . (*presses
a button*) You're still in the running . . . Yes
. . . Yes . . . OK . . . Just a mo. (*presses a
button*) Charlie, help me out on this one
. . . Good . . . I'm going to have to put you
on hold again . . . (*presses a button*) Have to
call you back . . . Final offer? . . . I don't
know . . . I'll get back to you . . . Promise.
(*presses a button*) Hi Charlie, congratulations
. . . Yep . . . OK . . . See you tomorrow
night . . . I guess that means I'm buying . . .
Bye.
(*he puts the phone down*)
(STEPHEN *has looked on at* ALEXANDER'*s
conversation in amazement, and now stares at
him, completely overwhelmed.*)

STEPHEN   So?
ALEXANDER   That's it.
STEPHEN   What?
ALEXANDER   250k.
STEPHEN   Two-hundred and fifty thousand?

ALEXANDER   Yep . . . The deal is done. They're sending the contract over in the morning . . . It's done.

STEPHEN   (*in disbelief*) It's done.

(ALEXANDER *gets up.*)

ALEXANDER   Congratulations. You are now officially a successful writer, with a three-book deal.

STEPHEN   Three books?

ALEXANDER   Don't worry about it. The next one isn't due until the end of next year. Plenty of time to get over your writer's block caused by all that money.

STEPHEN   I knew you could do it.

ALEXANDER   Without the book . . .

STEPHEN   Which you didn't like.

ALEXANDER   Which I didn't like.

STEPHEN   But that doesn't matter.

ALEXANDER   250k, three book deal.

STEPHEN   Film rights to come.

ALEXANDER   And paperback.

STEPHEN   I knew you could do it.

(ALEXANDER *and* STEPHEN *stand awkwardly in the middle of the room. Finally* STEPHEN *makes a move towards* ALEXANDER *and the two hug.*)

(ALEXANDER *pats* STEPHEN's *back.*)

ALEXANDER   Well done.

STEPHEN   No, it's all you. Without you . . .

ALEXANDER   Don't mention it.

(*They let go of each other.*)

STEPHEN   No hard feelings?

ALEXANDER   Are you kidding?

STEPHEN   I'll better go. Tell Clare.

ALEXANDER   You do that. Send her my love.
             (STEPHEN *turns to go, is halfway out of the*
             door, when ALEXANDER *stops him.*)
             Haven't you forgotten something?
             (STEPHEN *doesn't understand.*) The nega-
             tives. (STEPHEN *smiles embarrassed.*)
  STEPHEN   Sure, of course.
             (STEPHEN *awkwardly retrieves the envelope*
             with the negatives from his case.)
             There's an extra set, just in case . . . I always
             get an extra set done at the time; it works
             out cheaper than . . .
ALEXANDER   (*interrupts*) That's OK. (*takes the envelope.*)
  STEPHEN   I was never going to . . .
ALEXANDER   (*interrupts*) I know.
             (*They stand awkwardly.*)
  STEPHEN   I guess you better have some of these
             back . . . (*rummages though his bag, takes*
             copies of his book out) To send out.
ALEXANDER   Of course.
             (STEPHEN *awkwardly replaces the books on*
             the shelf, stands up when he's done.)
  STEPHEN   I guess that's it then.
ALEXANDER   I can't think of anything else.
             (STEPHEN *shakes* ALEXANDER'S *hand*
             enthusiastically.)
  STEPHEN   Bye.
ALEXANDER   We'll talk.
  STEPHEN   Thanks again.

             Finally STEPHEN *leaves the office, and*
             ALEXANDER *closes the door behind him.*

ACT II

He briefly flicks through the pictures, smiles wryly, then puts them one by one in the shredder.

He opens a cabinet and retrieves a bottle of expensive brandy and a glass. He pours himself a glass, sits down at his desk, puts the glass in front of him, but doesn't take a sip.

He presses a button on his telephone.

CHARLIE   (*on speakerphone*) Hello.

ALEXANDER   It's Alexander.

CHARLIE   (*on speakerphone*) Oh, hi. We were just talking about you. I'm glad you called. This book is really something. Marketing are really excited . . .

ALEXANDER   Look, I have a confession to make.

CHARLIE   (*on speakerphone*) Yes?

ALEXANDER   I lied to you.

CHARLIE   (on speakerphone, laughs) *You?* Lied to *me*? An *agent*?

ALEXANDER   Please . . . I'm serious.

CHARLIE   (*on speakerphone*) All right, let's hear it.

ALEXANDER   The book. I don't think . . .

CHARLIE   (*on speakerphone*) Yes?

ALEXANDER   I don't think it'll work.

CHARLIE   (*on speakerphone*) I disagree.

ALEXANDER   It's a bad book.

CHARLIE   (*on speakerphone*) I'm surprised, Alexander. You've actually read it?

ALEXANDER   I *loathe* the book.

CHARLIE   (*on speakerphone, laughs*) And?

ALEXANDER And . . . The writer . . .

CHARLIE (*on speakerphone*) Yes?

ALEXANDER The writer isn't an attractive, telegenic
woman exactly. He's more of your male,
nerdy kind of type.

CHARLIE (*on speakerphone*) Oh.

ALEXANDER Look . . .

CHARLIE (*on speakerphone*) What?

ALEXANDER I don't mind if you withdraw the offer.
After all I wasn't being entirely honest.

CHARLIE (*on speakerphone, disappointed*) I don't know
what to say.

ALEXANDER No hard feelings?

CHARLIE (*on speakerphone*) Well, it's going to make
things a little more difficult.

ALEXANDER Sure.

CHARLIE (*on speakerphone*) But to tell you the truth,
the book really *is* hot. I don't care if the
writer looks like a leper, this thing will sell
itself. (ALEXANDER *looks shocked.*) It's got
something. It really has. I must hand it to
you, you really stuck your neck out on
this.

ALEXANDER Look, Charlie. I need you to do me a
favour on this one.

CHARLIE (*on speakerphone*) Favour?

ALEXANDER Trust me on this.

CHARLIE (*on speakerphone*) I'm listening.

ALEXANDER Forget about it.

CHARLIE (*on speakerphone*) Forget about what?

ALEXANDER The book. Forget you ever read it.

CHARLIE (*on speakerphone*) Why?

ALEXANDER You owe me one.

CHARLIE	(*on speakerphone*) But . . .
ALEXANDER	Please.
	(ALEXANDER *waits anxiously.*)
CHARLIE	(*on speakerphone*) Forget about it?
ALEXANDER	Yes.
CHARLIE	(*on speakerphone*) But why? . . . Is there someone else?
ALEXANDER	No . . .
CHARLIE	Promise?
ALEXANDER	You have my word. It won't see the light of day.
CHARLIE	(*on speakerphone, sighs*) I don't know. This is a big favour to ask.
ALEXANDER	(*thinks*) Did I tell you we signed Jake?
CHARLIE	(*on speakerphone*) I knew it!
ALEXANDER	How would you like to get a first look at his new book?
	(*There's a pause as* CHARLIE *contemplates.*)
CHARLIE	(*on speakerphone, reluctant*) You're killing me.
ALEXANDER	Does that mean we have a deal?
	(*Short pause.*)
CHARLIE	(*on speakerphone*) Yes.
ALEXANDER	Thanks, I owe you one.

ALEXANDER *replaces the handset in the cradle.*

Finally he takes the glass of brandy. Immensely relieved, he takes a sip.

Darkness.

The Little Driver
Martin Wagner

2004 | paperback | 64 pages | ISBN 978-0-9530964-5-9

Joe always dreamt of driving his own car. When his wish comes true and he takes his brand-new sportscar for a spin through town and country, his adventures soon take a turn for the unexpected.

The Little Driver takes a fresh look at our obsession with cars through the eyes of a boy still young enough to take nothing for granted.

"Billed as 'An anti-car book for a new generation', *The Little Driver* is a gem, easily negotiating the many dead ends encountered when questioning car culture. Like many eight-year-old boys, Joe is obsessed with cars, but when his wish suddenly comes true he embarks on a journey he wasn't expecting. Full of wit and dry observation, much of the beauty of *The Little Driver* is in the way it captures the visceral thrill and smug pride Joe feels when first behind the wheel of his shiny red sports car, and then peels away the layers as Joe's encounters with selfish drivers, traffic jams, pollution and roadbuilding slowly force him to question his love of the automobile."

Andrew Brackenbury ERGO

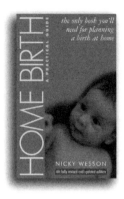

Home Birth
A Practical Guide
Nicky Wesson

2006 | paperback | 256 pages | ISBN 978-1-905177-06-6

A perfect balance of practical information, compelling personal
stories and research evidence, *Home Birth* is essential reading for all
couples considering the alternative to a hospital birth.
Leading childbirth educator Nicky Wesson dispels many common
myths about home birth and shows how having your baby in your
own home can be the most exciting and fulfilling thing you'll ever do.

"I have often thought about the problem of how do you tell a first-
time mum all that experience you pick up having babies, without
frightening her. How do you empower her to know what she
wants? This book goes a long way to solve the problem. It is written in a very easy to read, matter-of-fact way, interspersed with
heart-warming and heart-wrenching stories from other mums and
dads. A fabulous book – one of those that will go down in history
as a book that can change your life ... Don't miss reading it."

AIMS – Association for Improvements in the Maternity Services

Childbirth without Fear
The Principles and Practice of Natural Childbirth
Grantly Dick-Read
with a foreword by Michel Odent

2004 | paperback | 352 pages | ISBN 978-0-9530964-6-6

In an age where birth has often been overtaken by obstetrics, Dr Dick-Read's philosophy is still as fresh and relevant as it was when he originally wrote this book. He unpicks every possible root cause of western woman's fear and anxiety in pregnancy, childbirth and breastfeeding and does so with overwhelming heart and empathy. Essential reading for all parents-to-be, childbirth educators, midwives and obstetricians.

"Every pregnant mother should read it."
JANET BALASKAS – author of *New Active Birth*

"A brilliant, courageous classic."
INA MAY GASKIN – author of *Ina May's Guide to Childbirth*

Obedience to Authority
Stanley Milgram
foreword by Jerome Bruner

2005 | paperback | 256 pages | ISBN 978-0-9530964-7-3

Volunteers are invited to a scientific laboratory under the pretence
of participating in a study about the effects of punishment on learn-
ing. They are instructed by an experimenter to administer an electric
shock of increasing intensity to a 'learner' every time he makes a mistake. How many, if any, would go right up the scale to 450 Volts?
The implications of Stanley Milgram's extraordinary findings are dev-
astating. From the Holocaust to Vietnam's My Lai massacre, from
Bosnia to Iraq's Abu Ghraib prison, *Obedience to Authority* goes some
way towards explaining how ordinary people can commit the most
horrific of crimes if placed under the influence of a malevolent
authority.

"A masterpiece."

NEW STATESMAN

"Milgram's work is of first importance, not only in explaining
how it is that men submit, but also in suggesting how better
they may rebel."

SUNDAY TIMES

Irrationality
Stuart Sutherland

2007 | paperback | 256 pages | ISBN 978-1-905177-07-3

Why do doctors, generals, civil servants and others consistently make wrong decisions that cause enormous harm to others? And why do you sit through a boring play just because the tickets were expensive?

Irrational beliefs and behaviours are virtually universal. Not only gamblers and parapsychologists but selection committees and experts often fall into simple statistical traps to do with sample sizes or assuming causal links. In this iconoclastic book Stuart Sutherland analyses causes of irrationality and shows that it is universal. Drawing on a mass of intriguing research, he examines why we are irrational, the different kinds of irrationality, the damage it does us and the possible cures. He argues that we could reduce irrationality – but only if we first recognize how irrational we normally are.

"Terrifying, sometimes comic, very readable and totally enthralling." OLIVER SACKS

"Extremely gripping and unusually well written."
RICHARD DAWKINS